MEETING WISDOM™

Tap Into The Wisdom and Insight
of Thousands of 12 Step Meetings
in a Single Book

Brian L

Meeting Wisdom Publishing, Inc.
Los Gatos, CA
www.meetingwisdom.com

This book is dedicated to all those who are still suffering
and the kind souls who reach out to help them.

For information contact:
Meeting Wisdom Publishing
P.O. Box 320786, Los Gatos, CA 95032
info@meetingwisdom.com
www.meetingwisdom.com

First Printing 2002
ISBN 0-9718779-1-2
Library of Congress Card Number 2002103828

Publisher's Cataloging-in-Publication
(Provided By Quality Books, Inc.)

L., Brian, 1964-
    Meeting wisdom : tap into the wisdom and insight of thousands of 12 step meetings in a single book / Brian L. -- 1st ed.
    p. cm.
    Includes index.
    LCCN 2002103828
    ISBN 0-9718779-1-2

    1. Twelve-step programs--Quotations, maxims, etc.
    2. Recovering addicts--Quotations, maxims, etc.
    I.Title.

HV4998.L37 2002   616.86'06
                      QBI02-200266

This book was typeset using Adobe InDesign software. Typefaces used include Cataneo, Garamond, and Herculanum.

Table of Contents

About This Book...................................i

How To Use This Book....................ii

Share The Wisdom............................iii

Sayings & Wisdom............................1

Notes & Favorite Sayings.........160

The 12 Steps....................................165

The 12 Traditions.........................166

Excerpt From Pages 83-84.........167

A Few Suggestions......................168

More Wisdom & Resources.......169

Credits...173

Disclaimer

Proceed with caution – reading and use of the sayings and information in this book is at your own risk. It is not intended to provide medical, legal, psychological or any other form of personal or professional advice. The author and publisher shall have neither liability nor responsibility to any person or entity with respect to any loss or damage caused, or alleged to have been caused, directly or indirectly, by the information contained in the book or its use.

This book is not officially affiliated with Alcoholics Anonymous or any other 12 step group and is not AA conference approved literature. The views expressed are those of the author only.

Special thanks to Alcoholics Anonymous World Services.
The Twelve Steps and Twelve Traditions and a brief excerpt from the book, *Alcoholics Anonymous* are reprinted with permission of Alcoholics Anonymous World Services, Inc. ("A.A.W.S."). Permission to reprint the Twelve Steps and Twelve Traditions and the brief excerpt does not mean that A.A.W.S. has reviewed or approved the contents of this publication, or that A.A.W.S. necessarily agrees with the views expressed herein. A.A. is a program of recovery from alcoholism only - use of the Twelve Steps and Twelve Traditions and the brief excerpt in connection with programs and activities which are patterned after A.A., but which address other problems, or in any other non-A.A. context, does not imply otherwise.

Every effort has been made to attempt to locate the copyright owners of all material used. Because of the nature of this book, however, there are some quotations that are impossible to trace. We would be glad to hear from the legal copyright owners so that we can acknowledge and include them in future editions.

About This Book

I feel very lucky and very blessed to be sober and have a program of recovery that is working in my life. Through thoroughly working the Twelve Steps and attending meetings over the last decade I've been exposed to the stories and wisdom of hundreds of people with literally thousands of years of cumulative sobriety. This book is intended to share with you those things that have been so freely shared with me.

At one point in my recovery I realized that many of the wisest things people said at meetings would only stay with me for a short time. I would hear words of wisdom and they seemed practical and easy, yet a few days later I would forget them altogether and feel like I was back at square one. It was then that I decided to begin keeping a journal, with the goal of writing down the absolute best sayings, going far beyond the common ones (Easy Does It, One Day at a Time, etc.) to record the most useful and most profound.

My original intention was to capture these only for myself, but after I had quite a few sayings written down I realized that others could benefit from my efforts. From there I mentioned the idea to a few friends in the program and they wanted to get a copy so I decided to turn it into a book.

This book isn't a substitute for going to meetings or working the Twelve Steps and a good solid program. However, it is intended to help anyone in recovery - to supplement your other efforts and give you another tool to help you stay centered.

My hope in publishing this book is that it will help to expand the collective recovery wisdom in the world – that it will help others to find and maintain solid recovery and make people's lives more full of joy. And who knows…maybe it will help me for another twenty four hours too!

Brian L.
June 2002

How To Use This Book

There is no right or wrong way to use this book, but here are a few ideas to get you started:

- Read one saying per week and try applying it to your life.

- Open it anytime you are feeling good (or bad) to a randomly selected page and see what happens.

- Use the sayings as topics at meetings.

- Take it to meetings and write down your favorite sayings in the notes section in the back.

- Read it straight through. (you might want to stop and ponder each saying for a few minutes as you go)

- Sign up for the free weekly email version and see which sayings appear when you need them.

Notes:

1.) If the word God doesn't work for you simply cross it out and write in "Higher Power", "Nature", "Sam" or whatever else you like!

2.) Do the same with the word alcohol or alcoholic if you need to - write in "Addict", "Alanon" or whatever your addiction may be.

Wishing you all the best — happiness, joy and freedom!

Share The Wisdom

Our goal is to share this book with as many people as possible (even if they aren't in a 12 step program). That's why we are making the electronic version available for **FREE** at our website.

Help us share the wisdom:

- Write the next version with us! Email us your favorite sayings—if we include yours we'll give you a free copy.

- Tell your friends about the free electronic version - send them to our website to get it.

- Give it away!

    - Give a copy to a friend, Sponsor or Sponsee.

    - Make it a present for a sobriety birthday.

    - Send an anonymous copy to someone who needs it. (see the order form in the back)

- Forward your favorite sayings to friends via email.

Thanks for helping share the wisdom!

sayings@meetingwisdom.com
www.meetingwisdom.com

Sayings
&
Wisdom

No matter what...
I am always taken care of

യ

There are very few decisions that
cannot wait 24 hours

God is never late

Facts

can be stubborn things

If you go to meetings
        even when you don't need a meeting
you will rarely
need a meeting

When all else fails try God.

Or you can take the shortcut
and start with him.

Cooperating with God

is the easier softer way

Let go or be dragged...

If you reach out to someone

you just might save their life.

You never know.

Say what you mean

Mean what you say

But don't say it mean

Nothing ever goes
wrong in my life,

whether I know it

or not

Cultivate

Silence

Note to self:

Remember to
pray

My Higher

Power exists

☐Yes ☐No

It works better

if you get into the program

instead of

just getting around

the program

The people you most need to give love to

are often the people

who deserve it the least

Say,

"I Can Do That"

When you are

first getting sober,

trust people,

But

build trust

slowly

and carefully

If there is a God

He is probably

a lot smarter

than you are.

Why not let Him run the show?

Abstinence leads to sobriety.

*The program and 12 steps
    lead to recovery.*

Everything

is

going to be

All Right

If

you can't be happy

on a daily basis

then little else matters

Take a no BS
approach to
working your
program

The only one you have to

trust 100%

is God

I came from a dysfunctional family.

It was dysfunctional

because I was in it

and hadn't recovered yet

It's a daily program:
Yesterday's home run
may not be enough to
win the game today

Everything can go wrong
today and I will still be
okay

☏

Feelings

are nine times
more powerful
than intellect

*If you aren't enjoying
your life...*

*...then you
aren't recovering*

If you think you have a good
idea you might want to get
a second opinion from your
sponsor

(just in case) ☺

MEETING WISDOM
M
W

To judge whether an action is right or wrong,

imagine that after you have died

you describe the situation to God and say, "I'm
really sorry that I did that."

If you feel regretful then it is wrong – if not it
is probably okay

It really comes down to
one question:

"Will God always take care of me?"

The quality of the moment

equals

the quality of your life

I asked my sponsor

when it was going to start

getting better and he said,

"When you stop asking when
and start asking how"

Happiness
is pretty much
independent
of your
circumstances

If you wait around until you are
well enough to work the steps

you may never get started

Everyone here has

God

inside

of

them

Are you
finished
with fighting?

Almost everything

that happens

is no big deal

in the grand scheme of things

No matter what I do
or what choices I make

there are always

an unlimited number of
new and better possibilities

Me looking for

God

is like a fish looking for water

God or _____?

You can't run
from reality

*If you want what we have
and are willing to go to
any lengths to get it...*

...then keep coming back

Kindness

kills

resentment

Say,

"Thank You"

to the universe

I need

nothing more

than I

already have

You won't be entirely ready

to give up your defects of character

until you are willing to let go

of the benefits they give you

Do what you love

and happiness

will follow

Struggling

is

Optional

When faced with a problem
immediately ask,

"How is this a blessing?"

Welcome to the world's

largest organization of

members who started out

not wanting to be here

Many people delay the Fourth Step because they are waiting around for their past to get better before they begin writing

Unlikely things tend to stay unlikely.

If you have been unable to control
your drinking in the past

It is unlikely
that you will miraculously become
able to control it in the future

People
who don't come back to meetings
don't get the chance to find out
what happens to people
who don't
come back to meetings

If you are an alcoholic

you can probably control

your drinking

and not enjoy it

or enjoy your drinking

and not control it

Be proud of yourself,

No Matter What

Sometimes
the only thing I can
change is my attitude

Ironically,
that is all I ever really need
to change

God is never confused.

Define yourself
by what you do
and how you do it
rather than
by what you have

Be still.

Listen.

Hear.

Know.

"Thy Will Be Done"

...means not only what
happens to me

but what I
choose to do

You are either going

towards the light

or away from it

Humility
is the key to true long-term happiness

♥

Pray from the

center

of your heart

The problem is self...

The answer
is Spiritual

We are all here*

because we weren't all

there

* (in the progam)

If your problems aren't being

solved maybe your God is too

small

Honesty without kindness
is cruel.

Kindness without honesty
is codependence

Sponsor

someone who teaches you how to work the steps

Attitude

is far more important

than "facts"

Short prayer:

Thanks God,
and keep it coming

There are plenty of people

who are too smart
    to get the program,

but there is no one
    who is too stupid

For the most part,

happiness

has very little to do with

circumstances

Here in the program we'll

laugh at you until you can

laugh at yourself

(and love you until you can love yourself)

If I give up my denial what will I have left?

I've worried about lots of
things in my life

and a few of them have even
come true

∽

Whenever you have a problem

*you will always find your
fingerprints on it*

Life

is to be **enjoyed**
not endured

Relax.

There is plenty of time.

Without trust

life

isn't much worth

living

*S*on

*O*f a

*B*itch

*E*verything's

*R*eal

Be careful who you listen to:
People at meetings are not
known to be a bedrock of
mental stability

Being rich

without serenity

is worth less

Not knowing

isn't the problem

not being okay

with not knowing

is the problem

Every day make a list
of five things
you are grateful for.

No more, no less.

Some days it will be hard to
come up with five, some days it
will be hard to stop at five.

Have Faith.

No matter what happens

you can't (and won't) lose

Think,

"How can I do this?"

not,

"If I do this"

If you don't take the first drink

you can't get drunk

Instead of asking,

"Why am I an alcoholic?"

ask,

"What am I going to do
about it?"

My job:
Stay positive and optimistic and be
ready for good things to happen.

God's job:
Take care of the results

Make *serenity*
the focus of your life

God *always gives us the answers that we need when we are willing to listen*

God
is a verb

Pray for the willingness
to be willing
to be willing

to let go absolutely

We come into AA and
have to have blind faith

– over time it becomes
non-blind faith

Focus on

Really,

Really,

Really

loving God

Solve all of your

problems with

love

Trust

is something that must be earned.

If you aren't working

with others

then others

will be working with you

MEETING WISDOM M W

102

We can make the plans
but we can't
plan the results

2 question checkup:

1.) What step are you on?

2.) What's your sponsor's phone number?

Ask yourself

"What can I do

this moment

to have an awesome

day?"

I like the spirituality of the program

It's the not drinking that I have a problem with.

We Alcoholics

aren't slow learners...

we are slow accepters

Alcohol never

"made" me do anything

it "allowed" me

to do things

Today

I choose to work my

program

and be happy

Think think think

First things first

But for the grace of God

Live and let live

Easy does it

The only way

to be truly free

is to do those things
that you ought to do

because you want to do them

Right acting leads to right thinking

When I got to the

program I was a

problem thinker

You go to meetings

to give,

Not to take

When you see someone you dislike, say to yourself:

"God loves you and the rest of us are trying"

Think and feel,

then react.

Don't react and feel,

and then think

When you get hit by a train

it's not the caboose*
that kills you

it's the engine**

* (the last drink)
** (the first drink)

Trust

your inner voice

and take one step

at a time

The alcoholic
takes a drink

and then the drink
takes the alcoholic

There is no use waiting around for something that isn't going to happen

Short Prayer:

"Here we go God"

Don't compare your insides
with other people's outsides

CR

When I am in pain
it is because I need to
change

and I am either
afraid

or unwilling to do so

If you want to know

what your character defects are

look

at the people you dislike

Resentment is choosing
to not forgive someone
for an extended period
of time.

It's your choice

The truth will set you
free,

but first it will probably
piss you off

Lord,

please help me
to keep my mouth shut.

Guilt is the past.

Anxiety is the future.

Serenity is the present

When things are

Difficult to read,

Choose to read them

As good

Just

have

Fun

Peace

no matter what

*I used to feel
impending doom:*

*Now I feel
impending good*

Thanks to the program

CR

There is a reason for everything that happens

though you may not be able to see or understand it now (or ever)

Sometimes

the only way through it

is through it

Fear Not

Be as Kind
as you can be
Today

especially to yourself!

Seek *God* before anything else

A relaxed attitude
is the key to it all

Trust

God

Refuse
to let anyone
move you
     off center

Be glad

that God is in charge

and that you don't

have to carry the

burden

God's will for today is CHP:

Compassion,

Honesty,

and Patience

in all my dealings with people

*I've spent most of my life
being worried about
having enough,
when in the end
that won't be what matters*

Visualize yourself
getting out of
The Director's chair

Everything is a

blessing...

...trust that

all is for good

Humility

Not thinking less of yourself.

Thinking of yourself less often.

The only person
I can ever be better than

is the person I was yesterday

Holding on to resentments
is like taking poison

and expecting the other person to die—

Relax...

God is in charge

and all is well

Surrendering doesn't
mean giving up
because you are a bad person,

it means letting God do it
for you
because you want to be
a happy person

Now

is where God is

There isn't much reason

to get upset about

anything

If you are right
with God
then everything
will be okay

If I were to hire someone
to manage and run my life

would I choose me
or would I choose God?

Since I am Sober
I am Successful

Whenever you have a problem

Relax and focus on working the program

Watch how the problem magically solves itself.

Don't drink no matter what

Everything

written in this book

could be wrong

Everything

written in this book

might be right

Notes & Favorite Sayings

Take this book to meetings with you and write down your favorite sayings...

_____

_____

_____

_____

_____

_____

_____

_____

_____

_____

_____

_____

Notes & Favorite Sayings

Notes & Favorite Sayings

Notes & Favorite Sayings

Notes & Favorite Sayings

The 12 Steps Of Alcoholics Anonymous

Here are the steps we took, which are suggested as a program of recovery:

1.) We admitted we were powerless over alcohol—that our lives had become unmanageable.

2.) Came to believe that a power greater than ourselves could restore us to sanity.

3.) Made a decision to turn our will and our lives over to the care of God *as we understood Him.*

4.) Made a searching and fearless moral inventory of ourselves.

5.) Admitted to God, to ourselves, and to another human being the exact nature of our wrongs.

6.) Were entirely ready to have God remove all these defects of character.

7.) Humbly asked Him to remove our shortcomings.

8.) Made a list of all persons we had harmed and became willing to make amends to them all.

9.) Made direct amends wherever possible, except when to do so would injure them or others.

10.) Continued to take personal inventory and when we were wrong promptly admitted it.

11.) Sought through prayer and meditation to improve our conscious contact with God as we understood Him, praying only for knowledge of His will for us and the power to carry that out.

12.) Having had a spiritual awakening as a result of these steps, we tried to carry this message to alcoholics and to practice these principles in all our affairs.

Reprinted with permission of Alcoholics Anonymous World Services, Inc.

The 12 Traditions Of Alcoholics Anonymous

1.) Our common welfare should come first; personal recovery depends upon A.A. unity.

2.) For our group purpose there is but one ultimate authority — a loving God as He may express Himself in our group conscience. Our leaders are but trusted servants; they do not govern.

3.) The only requirement for A.A. membership is a desire to stop drinking.

4.) Each group should be autonomous except in matters affecting other groups or A.A. as a whole.

5.) Each group has but one primary purpose—to carry its message to the alcoholic who still suffers.

6.) An A.A. group ought never endorse, finance or lend the A.A. name to any related facility or outside enterprise, lest problems of money, property and prestige divert us from our primary purpose.

7.) Every A.A. group ought to be fully self-supporting, declining outside contributions.

8.) Alcoholics Anonymous should remain forever nonprofessional, but our service centers may employ special workers.

9.) A.A., as such, ought never be organized; but we may create service boards or committees directly responsible to those they serve.

10.) Alcoholics Anonymous has no opinion on outside issues; hence the A.A. name ought never be drawn into public controversy.

11.) Our public relations policy is based on attraction rather than promotion; we need always maintain personal anonymity at the level of press, radio and films.

12. Anonymity is the spiritual foundation of all our traditions, ever reminding us to place principles before personalities.

Reprinted with permission of Alcoholics Anonymous World Services, Inc.

Excerpt From Pages 83-84

The following excerpt, found on pages 83-84 of the book *Alcoholics Anonymous*, describe what some people in the program refer to as "The Promises" that working the first nine steps will bring to the alcoholic or addict's life.

"If we are painstaking about this phase of our development, we will be amazed before we are half way through. We are going to know a new freedom and a new happiness. We will not regret the past nor wish to shut the door on it. We will comprehend the word serenity and we will know peace. No matter how far down the scale we have gone, we will see how our experience can benefit others. That feeling of uselessness and self-pity will disappear. We will lose interest in selfish things and gain interest in our fellows. Self-seeking will slip away. Our whole attitude and outlook upon life will change. Fear of people and of economic insecurity will leave us. We will intuitively know how to handle situations which used to baffle us. We will suddenly realize that God is doing for us what we could not do for ourselves.

Are these extravagant promises? We think not. They are being fulfilled among us—sometimes quickly, sometimes slowly. They will always materialize if we work for them."

Reprinted with permission of Alcoholics Anonymous World Services, Inc.

A Few Suggestions...

Here a few of the suggestions that helped to keep me sober and to bring recovery into my life.

Take what you like, leave the rest.

1.) Go to 90 meetings in 90 days. If you do this you will end up finding at least a few meetings you like and few people that you look forward to seeing.

2.) Read the book *Alcoholics Anonymous* (often referred to as the Big Book). The first 164 pages explain the program of recovery and are designed to "help you find a power greater than yourself that will solve your problem". The rest of the pages have stories that provide hope and inspiration.

3.) Read the book *Twelve Steps and Twelve Traditions* (often referred to as the 12 by 12). This book further explains the 12 Steps and 12 Traditions and can help you work a stronger program.

4.) Don't try to do the program alone. Get a sponsor who has worked all 12 steps and has what you want. Ask them to teach you how to work the steps.

5.) Choose a home group and go to it all the time!

6.) At every meeting try to introduce yourself to at least one person, get at least one phone number, and remember at least 2 people's names. Call one person per day.

7.) Don't drink or use no matter what happens!!!

More Wisdom & Resources

Here are a few of the resources we have found to be valuable for recovery. Check our website (www.meetingwisdom.com) for a more comprehensive list. Email us at info@meetingwisdom.com if there are others you feel should be listed!

Organizations

Alcoholics Anonymous (AA)
World Services, Inc.
Grand Central Station
PO Box 459
New York, NY 100163
212-870-3400
www.alcoholics-anonymous.org

Al-Anon/Alateen Family Group
Headquarters, Inc.
1600 Corporate Landing Parkway
P.O. Box 862
Virginia Beach, VA. 23454-5617
800-344-2666
WSO@al-anon.org
www.al-anon-alateen.org

Cocaine Anonymous (CA)
3740 Overland Avenue, Suite G
Los Angeles, CA 90034
800-347-8998
310-559-5833
cawso@ca.org
www.ca.org

Co-Anon Family Groups World
Services (for friends and family of
cocaine addicts)
PO Box 12722
Tucson, AZ 85732-2722
520-513-5028
www.co-anon.org

CoDA (Co-Dependents Anonymous)
Co-Dependents Anonymous World
Service, Inc.
PO Box 7051
Thomaston, GA 30286-0025
wscoda@alltel.net
www.codependents.org

Debtors Anonymous
General Service Office
PO Box 920888
Needham, MA 02492-0009
781-453-2743
781-453-2745 (Fax)
new@debtorsanonymous.org
www.debtorsanonymous.org

Dual Recovery Anonymous
World Service Central Office
P.O. Box 218232
Nashville, TN 37221-8232
877-883-2332 (Toll Free)
615-673-7677 (Fax)
www.draonline.org

Gamblers Anonymous
International Service Office
P. O. Box 17173
Los Angeles, CA 90017
213-386-8789
isomain@gamblersanonymous.org
www.gamblersanonymous.org

More Wisdom & Resources

Marijuana Anonymous
P. O. Box 2912
Van Nuys, CA 91404
800-766-6779
office@marijuana-anonymous.org
www.marijuana-anonymous.org

Narcotics Anonymous (NA)
World Service Office in Los Angeles
PO Box 9999
Van Nuys, California 91409
818-773-9999
818-700-0700
fsmail@na.org
www.na.org

**National Clearinghouse for Alcohol
and Drug Information**
P.O. Box 2345
Rockville, MD 20847-2345
800-729-6686
info@health.org
www.health.org

**RCA (Recovering Couples
Anonymous)**
P.O. Box 11029
Oakland CA 94611
510-663-2312
info@recovering-couples.org
www.recovering-couples.org
(Sometimes this group is open to all 12-
step fellowship issues, and sometimes it
is closed to sexual issues. Ask about the
purpose of the local group.)

SAA (Sex Addicts Anonymous)
PO Box 70949
Houston, TX 77270
713-869-4902 (or 1-800-477-8191)
info@saa-recovery.org
www.sexaa.org

SA (Sexaholics Anonymous)
PO Box 111910
Nashville, TN 37222
615-331-6230
saico@sa.org
www.sa.org

**SLAA (Sex and Love Addicts
Anonymous)**
The Augustine Fellowship.
P.O. Box 338
Norwood, MA, 02062-0338
781-255-8825
General-Questions@slaafws.org
www.slaafws.org

More Wisdom & Resources

OTHER RESOURCES:

www.aagrapevine.org
The AA Grapevine, the International Monthly Journal of Alcoholics Anonymous, is an integral part of the AA Fellowship and serves as a mirror to AA's development.

www.hazelden.org
info@hazelden.org
1-800-257-7810 (651-213-4000 outside the U.S.).
Hazelden is a non-profit organization providing high quality, affordable rehabilitation, education, prevention, and professional services and publications in chemical dependency and related disorders.

www.mentalhelp.net
Mental Help Net is a comprehensive source of online mental health information, news and resources. It is a free service to the worldwide mental health community of professionals and laypeople.

www.meetingwisdom.com

BOOKS:

Alcoholics Anonymous : The Story of How Many Thousands of Men and Women Have Recovered from Alcoholism-*Big Book edition*
By Alcoholics Anonymous

The Annotated AA Handbook : A Companion to the Big Book
by Frank D.

Twelve Steps and Twelve Traditions
by Alcoholics Anonymous

As Bill Sees It : The A.A. Way of Life...Selected Writings of A.A.'s Co-Founder

More Wisdom & Resources

Blueprint for Progress
by Alanon Family Group Headquarters Staff

It Works : How and Why : The Twelve Steps and Twelve Traditions of Narcotics Anonymous
by World Service Office

Narcotics Anonymous (Basic Text)
By World Service Office

Hope, Faith & Courage : stories from the fellowship of Cocaine Anonymous

Hope and Recovery : A Twelve Step Guide for Healing from Compulsive Sexual Behavior

Currency of Hope
by Debtors Anonymous

Life With Hope: A Return to Living Through the Twelve Steps and Twelve Traditions of Marijuana Anonymous
By A New Leaf Publications

Sex and Love Addicts Anonymous
by Augustine Fellowship Staff

For an even more comprehensive and up-to-date list of resources and recommended books check our website. You can also order any of the above books directly from at **www.meetingwisdom.com.**

Credits

It would be impossible to list all of the people, both living and passed away, who contributed to this book, and even more impossible to give them due thanks for what they have contributed to my life. Here are just a few of the names – if I forgot yours let me know next time I see you at a meeting...

Tom C, Chuck L, Frank A, Bob S, Little Eddie, Steve H, Kevin K, Joe C, Larry C, Pat G, Mark, Andre, Fred A, Willy, Brenda, Don, Jay, Ken, Bud T, Louetta, Pat, Johnny O, Kevin, Kevin H, Gwen, Dennis, Sarah V, Michael S, Herman R, Jack C, Terry, Bill V, JD, Nicky, John S, Ron, Jaymz, DJ, CathyAnn, Dwight, Bob, Nicky, Bob, Lane, Juanita, Jamie, Peggy, Nick, Don, Jamie, Mark, Jeff, Jim the electrician, Sheila M, Glenn, Dave A, Big John, Dr. Dave, Andrew, Scott P, Jean, Bill, Juanita, Gene, Susan, George, Ralph, Dan, Jim P, Bajen, Patty, Mark, Greg L, Bob W, Bill W, Bob S, Ed, Gwen, Linda, Stu, Harry, Susie, Esther, Dave, Jim, Melvin, Marilyn, Christine, Miranda, Michael, Ruth, Al, Dr. Bob, Jamie, Bob, Deanne, Jonathan, Melissa, Larry, Allen, Landon, John, Terri, Ed, Pat, Cliff, Jolly, Dave, Jimmy, Lou, Missy, Don, Andrea, Penny, The Saratoga Family Group, Juanita, Mark, Greg, Sarah, Christine, Dr. Bob, Rick, Stacy, Tom, Janice, Michelle, Lloyd, Will, Nick, Austin, Deeann, Jeff, Carlos, Estelle, Lisa, Stu, Peggy, Jamie, Jack, Larry, Roger, Janet, KC, Lance, Mark, Dave, Brad, Sean, Bob, Rob, Steve, Mole, Marc, Janie, Tristan, Chuck, Sierra, Erin, Zan, Dr. Ralph, Dr. Jim, Arvin, Bob F, Douglas, Bill F, Arlen, Richard, Jerry, Ron, Forrest, George K., Lucy, Nikki, Dell, Luis, Tracy, Winnie, Bob, Troy, Kay, Merdeth, Janus, Stephanie, Micky, Shirley, Sylvia, Chalk, Richard, John, Neil, Steve, Marge, Chuck, Marge, Jack H, George, The Grapevine Speakers Group, Don, Cory, George, Marianne, Al, Barbara, Under The Bridge Don, Shorty, Dr. Jack, Jimmy, Julie, Carol, Donnie, Jim, Bernice, Austin, Phil, Ted, Nancy, Jim, Easier Way Group, John, Ruth, Parry, David, Richard, Eva, Vanessa, Luis, Roger, Darryl, Will, Hugo, Rudy, Michelle, Howard, Asilomar Men's Retreat, Marlene, Channelle, Matt, Sheila, John, Janice, Tom, Lila, Melvin, Chris, Lou, Chris, Joe C, Linda, Brenda, Spencer, Robert, Sylvia, Gretchen, Jorge, Richard, Frank, Alan, Robert, Serenity at Noon Group, Gene, Dick, Channing, Joe, Fidel, Orlan, Julian, Bob, Bill, Dan, Jim, John, Buck, Bill, Jerry, Allen, Bob, Charlie, Patty, Charlie, Jim, Doug, Lynn, Jim, Mark, Paul, Ray, Al, Tom, John, Dan, Chuck C, Tom, Lucy, John S, Troy, Sarah, Don D, Willie, Travis, Gene, LG Men's Big Book Group, Nickie, Meredith, Judy A, Bill, Dena, Jay, Mary S, Virginia, Johnnie, Maria, Rich, Scott, Ben, Ray, Luis and many, many others...

Many thanks to Cathyann Fisher of Amethyst & Emerald Publishing (http://www.amethystandemerald.com). Without her coaching and inspiration this book would never have seen the light of day.

Many thanks also to Andrew Ogus (andrewogus@mindspring.com) for the cover design—one of the most talented designers I've had the privilege of working with.

Most of all I want to thank my Wife, Family and Friends for supporting me in making this happen. You make me feel like the luckiest man alive.

Index

Acceptance
6, 9, 10, 13, 18, 23, 29, 40, 52,
61, 87, 107

Amends
11, 18, 25

Anger
15, 18, 100, 125, 126, 148

Anxiety
4, 14, 15, 23, 29, 34, 40, 53, 128,
133, 138

Attitude
7, 10, 12, 13, 17, 24, 19, 25, 28,
31, 37, 52, 60, 73, 76, 90, 93,
100, 105, 109, 111, 113, 131,
136, 138, 142, 152

Challenge
15, 18, 19, 23, 29, 79, 41, 53

Change
6, 22, 40

Control
9, 10, 21, 26, 34, 52, 56, 58, 91,
144

Courage
8, 19, 23, 29, 38, 55, 123, 134

Denial
6, 45, 56, 78, 84, 120

Dependence
15, 21, 26, 71

Depression
13, 18, 22, 23, 24, 29, 31, 34, 37,
105, 133

Doubt
13, 15, 19, 23, 29, 34, 40, 63,
70, 133

Facts
6, 22, 25, 45, 73, 80, 84

Faith
3, 8, 9, 13, 15, 16, 21, 26, 34, 44,
53, 61, 87, 89, 98, 129, 133, 135,
139, 145

Fear
13, 15, 16, 23, 26, 29, 36, 38, 40,
52, 55, 70, 79, 123, 133, 135

Feelings
13, 14, 18, 23, 29, 30, 35, 116,
128, 132

Finances
13, 23, 49, 51, 86, 122, 137, 143

Forgiveness
10, 18, 60, 62

Fourth Step
6, 3, 55, 72, 108

Index

Freedom
9, 21, 41, 64, 110, 132

Frustration
13, 15, 29, 52

Gratitude
13, 48, 49, 51, 88

Growth
12, 17, 19, 22, 25, 36

Guidance
4, 9, 26, 32, 33, 36, 44, 53, 63,
68, 90, 112

Guilt
15, 23, 29, 33, 128, 150, 153

Happiness
7, 10, 24, 31, 35, 37, 40, 51, 59,
66, 76, 81, 105, 109, 132, 150

Higher Power
5, 8, 9, 15, 16, 21, 26, 34, 39,
40, 42, 44, 61, 70, 74, 93, 95,
96, 99, 137, 139, 141, 149, 151,
153, 154

Honesty
6, 25, 45, 71, 80, 120, 126, 142

Hope
5, 13, 16, 19, 23, 29, 41

Humility
9, 14, 28, 48, 62, 66, 146, 147

Inventory
6, 32, 147, 153

Laughter
24, 31, 51, 77, 115, 130

Letting Go
5, 9, 10, 16, 21, 40, 44, 50, 52,
93, 97, 103, 141, 144, 150

Love
11, 12, 18, 47, 51, 77, 99, 100,
114, 136

Meetings
7, 11, 46, 54, 57, 77, 114

Pain
6, 10, 17, 23, 29, 53, 133

Patience
4, 5, 12, 15, 18, 28, 49, 61, 87,
134, 142

Planning
4, 5, 21, 103

Prayer
8, 15, 44, 61, 67, 74, 121, 127

Index

Pride
17, 51, 59, 62, 75, 118, 146, 147

Progress
5, 7, 17, 19, 28, 36, 38, 65, 69, 92, 147

Relaxing
3, 14, 41, 63, 82, 94, 105, 110, 131, 132, 138, 141, 149, 152, 156

Resentment
10, 18, 47, 100, 124, 125, 148

Resources
169-172

Responsibility
6, 11, 36, 64, 80, 91, 92, 112, 116

Sanity
10, 15, 22, 29, 69, 85

Serenity
86, 94, 128, 131, 138, 140, 151, 152

Silence
14, 41, 63, 95, 127

Sponsorship
11, 32, 36, 72, 102, 104, 114

Steps
15, 17, 22, 25, 38, 46, 55, 72, 104, 109, 118, 156

Surrendering
6, 8, 9, 10, 16, 21, 26, 34, 40, 41, 45, 52, 87, 93, 150

Success
13, 17, 19, 31, 35, 36, 41, 49, 51, 81, 89, 122, 143, 155

Trust
3, 4, 8, 10, 16, 20, 21, 23, 26, 29, 34, 61, 83, 101, 118, 133, 139, 145

Will
10, 15, 23, 40, 64, 150

Willingness
7, 9, 10, 15, 17, 21, 25, 38, 50, 95, 97, 111

Working With Others
11, 12, 38, 72, 85, 102, 114

Quick Order Form

Ordering Meeting Wisdom and other books from us is easy!

1.) Web: www.meetingwisdom.com
2.) Mail: Meeting Wisdom Publishing, Inc. P.O. Box 320786 Los Gatos, CA 95032
3.) Phone: 408-374-6257 or toll free at 1-866-STEPS12 Have a credit card ready.
4.) Email: orders@meetingwisdom.com

Ordering information:

_____ copies of Meeting Wisdom @ $16.95 each $_____

Sales tax (CA residents only): $1.40 per copy (8.25%) $_____

Shipping: U.S. $4 for the first book, $2 for each additional copy $_____
          Int'l $9 for the first book, $5 for each additional copy

TOTAL $_____

Payment method (circle one):   Check   Money Order   MasterCard   Visa

Name on card:_____

Card number:_____ Exp. Date:_____

Shipping information:

Name_____

Address_____

City_____ State_____ Zip_____

Telephone_____

Email address_____

❑ Put me on your mailing list   ❑ Sign me up for free weekly Meeting Wisdom
   Note: we will never sell or rent your name or information to anyone.

Is this a gift? ❑ Yes ❑ No
If so, do you want this sent: ❑ Anonymously ❑ From_____

Short Message to be included_____

_____

Thank you for your order!

Quick Order Form

Ordering Meeting Wisdom and other books from us is easy!

1.) Web: www.meetingwisdom.com
2.) Mail: Meeting Wisdom Publishing, Inc. P.O. Box 320786 Los Gatos, CA 95032
3.) Phone: 408-374-6257 or toll free at 1-866-STEPS12 Have a credit card ready.
4.) Email: orders@meetingwisdom.com

Ordering information:

_____ copies of Meeting Wisdom @ $16.95 each $_____

Sales tax (CA residents only): $1.40 per copy (8.25%) $_____

Shipping: U.S. $4 for the first book, $2 for each additional copy $_____
       Int'l $9 for the first book, $5 for each additional copy

TOTAL $_____

Payment method (circle one):   Check   Money Order   MasterCard   Visa

Name on card:_____

Card number:_____ Exp. Date:_____

Shipping information:

Name_____

Address_____

City_____ State_____ Zip_____

Telephone_____

Email address_____

❑ Put me on your mailing list   ❑ Sign me up for free weekly Meeting Wisdom
    Note: we will never sell or rent your name or information to anyone.

Is this a gift? ❑ Yes ❑ No

If so, do you want this sent: ❑ Anonymously ❑ From_____

Short Message to be included_____

_____

Thank you for your order!